Responding to School Shootings:
A comparative analysis of four cases in the late 20th century

Corrin Riley
Independent Research
January 31, 2015

I would like to thank University of Delaware for helping me get started in the field of social science research. This project was started to gain experience in research for possibly continuing my education towards a doctorates. As time went on, I realized I enjoyed doing the work. Thank you for helping me realize where I could be beneficial in the criminal justice field.

I would also like to give mention to American Criminal Justice Association- Lambda Alpha Epsilon. An abbreviated version of this report was published in the LAE Journal this past year. I would like to thank Fred Campbell (Editor) for helping me finalize this report due to graduating before I was done.

Abstract

The responses of four school shooting events in the latter 20th century are examined. The purpose is to determine if responses are coordinated by first responders before any emergency management system is implemented. The responses are compared, and improvements demonstrated with each event. The final event leads into an introduction of incident command system (ICS).

Responding to School Shootings

Table of Contents

Responding to School Shootings

Introduction

This paper is a qualitative analysis that describes, and examines, the responses to four cases of the late 20th century (1966-1999). The purpose is to determine if responses are coordinated by first responders before any emergency management system is implemented. The purpose of this analysis is to look at who responds, how they respond, and whether there is a pattern in the response resembling ICS. The schools/colleges examined are University of Texas at Austin (1966), Grover Cleveland Elementary School (1979), Cleveland Elementary School (1989), and Columbine High School (1999).

The definition of school shooting has been a subject of debate by many scholars who study the phenomenon. It appears to be a combination of the terms spree killing, spree shooting, and mass murder. Rampage is a subcategory of mass murder, but motive plays a greater role, and is victim specific. School shooting (also known as rampage school shooting) has three basic components. Shootings mostly committed by adolescents. They occur at school, or a school-related place. The perpetrator is usually a current or former student. The question of the number and type of victims still exist, so it is left to the researcher's discretion. (Bockler et al 2013; Harding et al 2002; Newman et al 2004) For this analysis, all the cases have more than one victim either injured or killed.

Methodology

The paper is divided into four sections: incident overview, response, comparison, and introduction to ICS. The overview summarizes the four shooting events. The information is gathered from articles printed in local newspapers the day of the incident (if possible), or the day after. The reason for choosing local newspapers from the areas of the occurrences is the idea they are more accurate due to proximity. The information includes: what happens, who is the shooter, weapons that are found, how many are hurt or killed, and how it ends.

In the process of selecting the cases for analysis, the first case (1966) is preselected by an outside source. The remaining cases are selected to represent each of the decades in the late twentieth century. The criterion used is it occurs in schools, fits the definition of mass shooting, and it occurs in a decade representing the latter part of the twentieth century.

The response section is completed using information gathered from documents supplied by the lead responding agency, articles, documentaries, and books. Gathering this information is a little tougher because of the involvement of police agencies, and the information for one case is still in use. The information extracted from the documents is who responds, how long it takes to respond after the shooting starts, what actions are taken by emergency responders, what is the duration of the response, and how it ends.

Patterns, or improvements, found in the responses are noted in the comparison section. The comparison should show similarities and differences in the responses, and if there is a set standard in place for responding to mass shootings before the national implementation of the incident command system (ICS). Emergency responders are already being trained to do certain things, at certain times, and in a certain way.

The final section will introduce the ICS system that is used today. It will explain the system, and its components. The laws and directives responsible for ICS will be mentioned.

Incidents

On August 1, 1966 in Austin, Texas Charles Whitman goes to the tower observation deck at University of Texas at Austin and open fires on the civilians below. Before the rampage begins, he murders his mother and wife. On the way up to the deck, he bludgeons a receptionist, murders two people descending from above, and wounds two others. Once on the deck, Whitman open fires with multiple weapons on crowds below, and on nearby streets. Two officers who make it to the deck kill him. Afterwards, there are sixteen dead and thirty-two wounded. The motive is never discovered. (Barr, 2013)

In the early morning of January 29, 1979 in San Diego, California Brenda Ann Spencer takes a .22 caliber semiautomatic rifle and open fires on a schoolyard across the street from her home. The school, Grover Cleveland Elementary School, is just getting started as students are arriving. After the rampage, there is a six hour standoff with police until she finally surrenders. In the end, two adults die, and nine are wounded. Spencer's motive is, supposedly, because she did not like Mondays. (Wolf, 1989)

In the afternoon hours of January 17, 1989 in Stockton, California a drifter open fires on a schoolyard. The school, Cleveland Elementary School, is just starting recess for 300 plus students from first to third grade. While wearing battle gear, Patrick Edward Purdy enters the schoolyard armed with several weapons, including an AK-47 and a 9mm pistol, and starts spraying the area with bullets. At one point during the shooting, his car explodes into a fireball. There are five children killed, and 31 children and adults wounded. The children who are able to flee inside are kept behind locked doors until parents arrived. The motive is never discovered, and the shooter commits suicide. (Curslidge 2009; Kempsky et al 1989; Staff, 1989)

On April 20, 1999 in Littleton, Colorado, two gunmen take over Columbine High School. Eric Harris and Dylan Klebold start the approximately four-hour rampage by throwing an explosive onto the roof of the school during the first lunch break. They fire on the people below. After entering the building from the roof, they fire at students and teachers in the cafeteria. As they proceed to the library Harris and Klebold spray the hallways with bullets, shoot at people, and place explosives around the building and bodies. There are two cars in the parking lot that contain explosives, and one of the gunmen has explosives strapped on. In the library students and teachers are shot, some for being black or praying. The nightmare ends with the gunmen killing themselves. One home search reveals more explosives. The motive is unclear because there is a mix of theories. (Obmascik, 1999)

Response

In this section, the responses are covered separately. This is to introduce how each case is responded to, and provides more details. A timeline for each case was presented in appendix B for clarity.

Responding to School Shootings

In the 1966 case at the University of Texas at Austin the first responders are campus security, Austin Police Department, Texas Highway Patrol, and the Texas Rangers. Many civilians with deer rifles assist them. One civilian flies a sharpshooter over the tower, but retreats after receiving shots fired. There is one person, a retired air force and army pilot, who volunteers to ascend the tower with a team of officers. There is no clear line of authority, and it is assumed that Austin Police Department is in charge. Even the students are acting on their own to rescue the injured. (Martinez 2005:65-90; Helmer 2000:113-130; Recer 1966:3; Herald Tribune 1966:9; Recer 1966: 1&2)

The shooting from the tower starts at 11:48am. There are already five fatalities by this time (shooter's mother and wife, the tower receptionist, and two visitors in the tower). The campus security is notified immediately, but it takes four minutes before Austin Police Department receives report of the shooting. At noon, the students could hear approaching sirens, but many are still unaware of what is happening. The doctor on call is summoned to the tower to treat the wounded five minutes after noon, but it is too dangerous to approach the tower. It is not until 12:23pm when police and civilians alike get frustrated due to the ineffectiveness of the police issued weapons, and go home to retrieve their own deer rifles. They fire at the shooter, but their own weapons prove to be on little help. It does not help that the shooter is a trained military sniper. At 12:35pm an armored vehicle is finally permitted on campus to retrieve the wounded and deceased as shots are still being fired. It takes the initiative of a couple trained officers, and a military trained civilian, to end the shooting by ascending the tower to ambushing the shooter. During their ascent, a sharpshooter tried to kill the shooter from a plane, but has to retreat when fired upon. An hour and forty-three minutes after the shooting begins, the shooter is killed. They use a white towel to stop the gunfire from below. (Martinez 2005:65-90; Helmer 2000:113-130)

It should be noted that the phenomena of school shootings emerges with this case. There have been some advancements due to the case, like the creation of the University of Texas Police Department, Special Weapons and Tactical unit, and the Active Shooter Response Team. (Martinez 2005:65-90; O'Toole 2013:177)

In the 1979 case, San Diego Police Department is the only responding agency due to its large size. Of course, it helps that the shooting stops before they arrive. The shooting, supposedly, starts at 8:30am as the children are entering the school after the first bell. The shots are coming from a home across the street from the school. Shots are fired for 20 minutes killing two people. At one point, a security guard from the nearby high school, where the children are later bussed to, arrives to help the officers on scene. He helps move a large vehicle into the line of fire so they could create a barrier to protect the children as they get on busses to be evacuated. SWAT team members are positioning themselves on roofs, and in yards, to be ready if they need to kill the shooter. It turns out the firing stops because the phone is ringing, and the shooter answers. It is a reporter assigned to the story trying to gather information on the shooter. Little does he know the first number he dials belongs to the home of the shooter. (Fast 2013:253-255; The Evening Independent 1979: 2A; YouTube N.d.:1-5)

The time of reporting the shooting to police is presumably ten minutes after the shooting starts. Ten minutes later, the shooting stops after 36 rounds are fired, and eleven people have been hit. This appears to be just as the police arrive because they proceed to evacuate homes at the time. At nine a.m. a six in a half hour standoff ensues. It is not until noon when the negotiator makes first contact because a reporter is on the line, and then the phone is off the hook. It takes three hours, and several hang-ups, before a rapport is established between the negotiator and shooter. At the same time the SWAT members are preparing to launch tear gas canisters into the house. Children and teacher are not evacuated from the school until 1:20pm after unknown delays. The members have to be relieved at several times due to built up anxiety. At the end, the shooter is arrested after surrendering to police, and the children are safely in their parent's arms. (Cannon 1979:A1&8; Clarke 1979:9; Cubbison 1979:A9; Fast 2013:253-255; Scott-Blair 1979:A9 Standefer 1979:A1&8)

Before the establishment of SEMS in 1994, a mandate of staff being response workers, teachers and staff are already acting as emergency responders. They are the true responders of the day. There is a slight delay in response by teachers because they thought the noise is from firecrackers. (Curslidge 2009)

On January 17, 1989 the response is quick. At about 11:40am a gunman, Patrick Edward Purdy, enters the schoolyard from the south side and open fires on 300 plus first through third grade students just starting recess. The school complex is set up like a complex with portable classroom buildings surrounding the main building where the cafeteria is housed. The playground is in the center of this complex. While standing next to the portable classroom at the far south end of the yard, Purdy fires multiple rounds into the crowd of playing students in a spraying motion. After firing 105 rounds from positions on both sides of a building, Purdy hears the police approaching and pulls out a 9mm pistol to use on himself. Rob Young, a first grader wounded in the leg and chest, believes the shooting lasted one and a half to two minutes. (Curslidge 2009; Kempsky et al 1989)

When the students and teacher in the classrooms realize what is happening they dive to the floor in cover. Some teachers take the students to a safer position in the halls. Children are being pulled inside as they run past classroom doors. The staff starts moving the children to the cafeteria in the center of the school. There is a small gap in the walkway between the classrooms and the cafeteria, so teachers and those who come to help form chained to protect the children. The cafeteria doors are locked to keep the children safe from onlookers and hysterical parents while they are checked out by medics and other first responders. The staff has to perform roster matchups to make sure the right child goes home with the right parent. One mother describes it as "organized mayhem." (Curslidge 2009)

The response by police is quick because the shooting ends just as local, federal, and county police arrive. They receive a call that shots are heard at 11:42am, according to Deputy Chief Lucian Neely. There is a command post established to coordinate response, investigation, and traffic control. The leading agency is the Stockton Police Department with assistance from Stockton Fire Department. By the time police respond, the shooter has already committed suicide after firing over 105 rounds. When they arrive, the activities are locating victims and getting them to area hospitals, locating the shooter and weapons, and securing the perimeter. (Johnson 2013; Kempsky et al 1989; Halvorson 1989.)

The 1999 case is when there appears to be more use of an organized response. There are several agencies involved at the local and federal level, state is conspicuously missing. The leading agency is the Jefferson County Sherriff's Office.

The whole response takes almost five in a half hours, even though the shooting lasts about 49 minutes. The response starts at 11:21am with a report of an explosion at a location near Columbine High School that turns out to be a diversion. The Littleton Fire Department is dispatched to respond at 11:26am. A minute after the call for the explosion, at Columbine High School, the students notice a commotion outside the cafeteria, and are distracted as a duffle bag containing an incendiary device is placed in the room. At 11:23am, there is a call from the high school to Jefferson County Sheriff's Office, and the first officer is on scene. He cannot enter the school because the shooters are still active, and calls for assistance as the shooting and explosions continue. Shots are heard in the library, and a fire alarm is activated. By 11:32am the request for mutual aid is sent out. (Pocsik 2000)

Jefferson County Sherriff's Office establishes a command post onsite at 11:36am, and a minute later Littleton Fire Department establishes a staging area at a nearby location. As the perimeter is being established around the school, the duffle bag in the cafeteria ignites starting a fire. Jefferson County and Arapahoe bomb squads are en route as ambulances wait for the wounded in the staging area. By noon a circling news helicopter is commandeered so the incident commander can survey the area, and an armored vehicle is used to retrieve the wounded. SWAT teams from Jefferson County, Denver, and Littleton use a fire truck to get near the school. They split into two teams with one entering from the east, and the other entering the from west. Littleton Fire Department and EMS rescue victims outside the cafeteria as police provide cover fire. A deputy spots students hiding behind cars, and works to evacuate them. (Pocsik 2000)

Eight minutes after noon the shooters commit suicide. The response continues because it is unknown whether there are any others, or more explosives. A triage area is established by Littleton Fire Department. A man that was spotted on the roof earlier is apprehended for questioning, but is later cleared by police. Another man is apprehended while approaching the school with a weapon, but is later cleared by police because he is found to be a civilian coming to help. In the staging area, the bomb squad (made up of six agencies) prepares to either go to the home of one shooter, or the school to assist in the response. A Special Operations Response Team (SORT) is dispatched at 12:30pm to a local elementary school to assist in evacuating its students, and prepare for incoming parents who are directed to go there. At 1pm the Jefferson County Critical Incident Shoot Team (CIST) is activated, and sharpshooters are placed on the roofs of neighboring homes. A SWAT team had to enter the school through a window because a bomb is found at the door. (Pocsik 2000)

After it is determined the shooters are dead, the SWAT teams start a general sweep to evacuate the school. Students are found hiding in the ceiling in the kitchen area. Others are found hiding in classrooms. One student is spotted hanging from a window. After all the students, faculty, and staff are evacuated, the bomb squad, and fresh SWAT teams are requested. There are two booby-trapped vehicles found in the parking lot as phase two of response begins. (Pocsik 2000)

During phase one a bomb squad at the home of one shooter has to call in Littleton Fire Department after smelling a gas odor. A bomb and gas can are discovered by Littleton Fire Department. Nearby homes are evacuated. The device is removed, and people return to their homes. (Pocsik 2000)

Comparisons

In comparing the responses of the four cases studied there seems to be gradual improvements. The cooperation is always there, but the coordination is lacking at first. This is demonstrated as the response in each case is discussed.

In the 1966 Austin, Texas incident the initial responders are the campus security officers, followed by the Austin Police Department, Texas Highway Patrol, and the Texas Rangers. There is no official coordination among the different departments, or among individual departments. It becomes every man for himself. Civilians and officers get fed up with the lack of progress, and go home to retrieve personal rifles. Once back on campus, they start shooting at the sniper. Any actions by legal officials are either slow, or independently organized. There is no set standard for response among departments

In the 1979 San Diego, California event there is coordination within department since the San Diego police are the only responders. There is a command post established. San Diego police officers were the only responders. In addition, this event occurs 14 years before the establishment of the Standardized Emergency Management System (SEMS) in California. The school district already has their own security, and an officer from a nearby high school does respond. The officers who respond for the San Diego department are forced into a standoff. There is coordination among the negotiator, SWAT, and patrol to control the situation.

In the 1989 Stockton, California case there is coordination among local, county, and federal police. It is five years before SEMS is activated. Because the shooter is already dead, the need for coordination is minimal.

In the 1999 Littleton, Colorado incident all responding departments coordinate very well. This is the first sign of incident command system (ICS) being used before its establishment, and may have set the standard. It appears the communication is not shared among departments, but each department may have spread the word through informal channels. Though there are responders from different cities, they all work together to achieve their assigned goals. Every step of the response from beginning to end is well coordinated and executed. There appears to be no jurisdictional issues. It still remains unclear if a set standard for response really exist.

Only true similarities are the fact that the shooter is stopped, and there is an official response by police. Each case shows improvement in coordination. Only one case shows use of a standard for response among agencies.

Introduction to ICS

The 1999 case is the only one to show the benefits of using the Incident Command System (ICS). There is coordination among multiple agencies after a statewide mutual aid is requested. There are sections, task forces, and divisions as found in an ICS chart.

Incident Command System (ICS) is a standardized, flexible, coordinated, on scene management concept that can fit any size event whether planned or not. It is born out of three mandates: National Framework Response (NFR), National Incident Management System (NIMS), and the National Preparedness Goal. (FEMA 2012) These mandates come from Homeland Security Presidential Directive five (HSPD-5) management of domestic incidents, and Homeland Security Presidential Directive eight (HSPD-8) national preparedness. (Bush 2003; Obama 2011)

This structure is created out of the business model. It is flexible because it could grow or shrink with the needs of the response. It calls on mutual aid to bring in resources from other jurisdictions, and they are managed under one command making it coordinated. The standardization comes from the system being used by all response agencies in the country. (FEMA 2012)

To further understand how ICS works the basic structure is explained. At the top is the incident commander (IC). This could be one person or a unified command (UC) of various agencies. The incident commander is responsible for the entire response, and does all the positions in the command structure until either response is over, or others are assigned to the positions. (FEMA 2012)

Under the incident commander (IC) there is a command staff comprised of a public information officer (PIO), liaison officer, and a safety officer. The PIO is responsible for gathering information to disseminate to stakeholders. The liaison officer is the middle person between command and assisting agencies. The safety officer is responsible for ensuring the safety of all response personnel. (FEMA 2012)

Under the command staff is the general staff. These are the people who direct the responders. The general staff includes four sections: operations, planning, logistics, and administration/finance. The operations section is responsible for directing and coordinating all tactical operations. The planning section creates the incident action plan (IAP), maintains the resource and incident status, develops alternative strategies, creates a demobilization plan, and provides documentation services and a primary location for representatives. The logistic section provides the resources needed to support response personnel and activities. The administration/finance section deals with contract negotiations and monitoring, timekeeping, cost analysis, and compensation for injured or damaged. (FEMA 2012)

Under each of these sections are divisions, groups, task force, strike teams, branches, and units. This is where the physical response takes place. Responders are divided into these categories for span of control so supervisors do not get overwhelmed. (FEMA 2012)

As shown in the 1999 case, this structure proves to be beneficial because every responding agency is on the same page as to what is going on. This is the complete opposite of the 1966 case where there is no way to know what the plan is, if there is one. ICS is the same line of authority used in businesses every day. If it could work there, why not work in response situations?

Conclusion

The purpose of this comparative analysis paper is to examine the responses to school shootings. There are four cases from the late 20th century, before the establishment of a national standard known as ICS. Those cases are 1966 University of Texas at Austin, 1979 Grover Cleveland Elementary School, 1989 Cleveland Elementary School, and 1999 Columbine High School.

Previous research is presented on school preparedness. The research demonstrates the vulnerability of our educational system. This brings the conclusion, schools do not have the capabilities to fully prepare for emergencies such as school shootings.

The response of each case is examined, and then compared to the other cases to determine if there are commonalities. The actions in each response are also examined to determine if a set standard is used before ICS. To get a better understanding of the acronyms used in responses they are discussed in appendix A. There is no set national, or state, standard for examined responses when they occur. Each department has their own procedures. The common goal of saving lives is what gets the job done.

The responses are unique to each case. Three of the cases present lessons learned to improve response. The final case is the capstone because much of what is done mimics ICS today.

References

"6 Die in School Shooting: Berserk Man in Satanic Garb Wounds 35 Others in Stockton: Shoots Self in the Head After Spree." 1989. *Los Angeles Times*, January 17. Retrieved January 19, 2013 (http://articles.latimes.com/1989-01-17/news/mm-695_1_stockton-elementary-school).

Barr, Alwyn. 2013. "Whitman, Charles Joseph." Austin, Texas: Handbook of Texas Online. Retrieved January 19, 2013 (http://www.tshaonline.org/handbook/online/articles/fwh42).

Biography. 2004. "Charles Whitman: Part 1 through 5." *YouTube*. Retrieved March 29, 2013 (http://www.youtube.com/watch?v=Y5Jc3zV6YO8&feature=g-list&list=PLz9IPo5JLXHGSmeX3rhcaKl5wCRJvpCaz).

Bockler, N., T. Seeger, P. Spitzer, and W. Heitmeyer. 2013. "School Shootings: Conceptual framework and international empirical trends." *School Shootings: International Research, Case Studies, and Concepts for Prevention, pp. 4-5.* New York: Springer.

"Brenda Spencer Faces 12 Charges in Shooting Spree." 1979. *The Madison Courier*, February 1, pp. B-5. Retrieved March 28, 2013 (http://news.google.com/newspapers?id=ontbAAAAIBAJ&sjid=6lANAAAAIBAJ&dq=brenda%20spencer&pg=3110%2C5276599).

Bush, George W. 2003. "Homeland Security Presidential Directive/HSPD-5- Management of Domestic Incidents: President's radio address." Government Publishing Office. Retrieved April 25, 2013 (http://www.gpo.gov/fdsys/pkg/PPP-2003-book1/pdf/PPP-2003-book1-doc-pg229.pdf).

California Emergency Management Agency. 2013. "Standardized Emergency Management System." Retrieved on March 20, 2014 (http://www.calema.ca.gov/PlanningandPreparedness/Pages/Standardized-Emergency-Management-System.aspx).

Cannon, Carl M. 1979. "The Schoolyard: Horror to some, show for others." *The San Diego Union*, January 30, A-1 & 8.

Clarke, Norm. 1979. "Stunned, Bewildered Students Wonder: Why did Brenda Spencer shoot at them?" *The Madison Courier*, January 31, pp. 9. Retrieved March 28, 2013 (http://news.google.com/newspapers?id=ontbAAAAIBAJ&sjid=6lANAAAAIBAJ&dq=brenda%20spencer&pg=5414%2C4755092).

Collins 2013. "English Dictionary." *Collins Dictionary Online.* Hammersmith, London: Collins Language Products. Retrieved February 22, 2013 (http://www.collinsdictionary.com/).

Cubbison, Gene. 1979. "Police Negotiator Was Instrumental in Ending Crisis at San Carlos." *The San Diego Union*, January 30, A-9.

Curslidge, Tara. 2009. "Dan Castillo." *The Record.* Retrieved November 27, 2013(http://www.youtube.com/watch?v=aGkmTGPS6-M&list=PLz9IPo5JLXHGSmeX3rhcaKl5wCRJvpCaz&index=14).

Curslidge, Tara. 2009. "Marianne Castillo." *The Record.* Retrieved November 27, 2013(http://www.youtube.com/watch?v=rRFxFvaVBEo&list=PLz9IPo5JLXHGSmeX3rhcaKl5wCRJvpCaz&index=15).

Curslidge, Tara. 2009. "Rann Chun." *The Record.* Retrieved November 27, 2013(http://www.youtube.com/watch?v=TGei9SOQr5o&list=PLz9IPo5JLXHGSmeX3rhcaKl5wCRJvpCaz&index=18).

Curslidge, Tara. 2009. "Rob Young." *The Record.* Retrieved November 27, 2013(http://www.youtube.com/watch?v=yAPKxyI9y-A&list=PLz9IPo5JLXHGSmeX3rhcaKl5wCRJvpCaz&index=19).

Curslidge, Tara. 2009. "Shannon Lopez." *The Record.* Retrieved November 27, 2013(http://www.youtube.com/watch?v=KoWOn797UHs&list=PLz9IPo5JLXHGSmeX3rhcaKl5wCRJvpCaz&index=12).

Curslidge, Tara. 2009. "Shirley Lopez." *The Record.* Retrieved November 27, 2013(http://www.youtube.com/watch?v=l4Mes_iAY5k&list=PLz9IPo5JLXHGSmeX3rhcaKl5wCRJvpCaz&index=13).

Fast, Jonathan. 2013. "Unforgiven and Alone: Brenda Spencer and Secret Shame." Pp. 253-255 in School Shootings: International Research, Case Studies, and Concepts for Prevention, edited by N. Bockler, T. Spencer, P. Sitzer, and W. Heitmeyer. New York: Springer.

FEMA. 2012. ICS 300: *Intermediate ICS for Expanding Incidents Student Manual*. Dover, Delaware: Delaware Emergency Management Agency.

FEMA. 2008. "Glossary."Pp. G1-G16 in ICS 300" Intermediate ICS for Expanding Incidents. Student Manual, edited by J. Schladen. Dover, Delaware: Delaware Emergency Management Agency.

"Five Children Killed as Gunman Attacks a California School." 1989. *The New York Times*, January 18. Retrieved March 30, 2013 (http://www.nytimes.com/1989/01/18/us/five-children-killed-as-gunman-attacks-a-california-school.html).

Halvorson, Shawn. 1989. "Cleveland School: January 17, 1989 Raw Video Footage of Aftermath." *YouTube.* Retrieved November 27, 2013(http://www.youtube.com/watch?v=a1dMhxbP_uY&list=PLz9IPo5JLXHGSmeX3rhcaKl5wCRJvpCaz&index=11).

Harding, D. J., C. Fox, and J. Mehta. 2002. "Studying Rare Events through Qualitative Case Studies: Lessons from a study of rampage school shootings." *Sociological Methods and Research*, 31(2), pp. 174-217.

Helmer, William, J. 2000. "The Madman on the Tower." Pp. 113-130 in Texas Crime Chronicles, edited by Texas Monthly. New York: Warner Brooks, Inc.

Johnson, Cliff. 2013. "Cleveland School Shooting- Case #89-2446 (Email Communication)." *Stockton Police Department Cold Case Unit.*

Kempsky, Nelson, Gary A. Blinkerd, Phil Yee, Allen Benitez, and Richard Yarvis. 1989. "A Report to Attorney General John K. Van De Kamp on Patrick Edward Purdy and the Cleveland School Killings." *California Department of Justice: Office of the Attorney General.* Retrieved November 27, 2013(http://www.schoolshooters.info/PL/Official_Reports_files/Purdy%20-%20official%20report.pdf).

Lavergne, Gary M. 1997. Gary M. Lavergne Papers: A Sniper in the Tower: Charles Whitman Collection (Photocopies). University of Texas at Austin: Dolph Briscoe Center for American History.

Martinez, Ramiro. 2005. *They Call Me Ranger Ray, pp. 65-90.* New Braunfels, Texas: Rio Bravo Publishing.

"Memories Still Vivid of the Madman on the Tower." 1986. *Lodi News Sentinel*, August 4, pp. 8. Retrieved March 28, 2013 (http://news.google.com/newspapers?id=4-IzAAAAIBAJ&sjid=nTIHAAAAIBAJ&dq=houston%20mccoy&pg=7010%2C4388325).

Newman, K. S., C. Fox, D. J. Harding, J. Mehta, and W. Roth. 2004. *Rampage: The Social Roots of School Shootings*. New York: Basic

O'Toole, Mary, Ellen. 2013. "Jeffrey Weise and the School Shooting at Red Lake Minnesota High School: A Behavioral Perspective." Pp. 177 in *School Shootings: International Research, Case Studies, and Concepts for Prevention*, edited by N. Bockler, T. Spencer, P. Sitzer, and W. Heitmeyer. New York: Springer.

Obama, Barack. 2011. "Presidential Policy Directive/PPD-8: National Preparedness." The White House. Retrieved April5, 2013 (http://www.dhs.gov/xlibrary/assets/presidential-policy-directive-8-national-prepa redness.pdf).

Obmascik, Mark. 1999. "High School Massacre Columbine Bloodbath Leaves up to 25 Dead: [Rockies Edition]." *The Denver Post*, April 21, pp. A-01. Retrieved January 21, 2013 (http://search.proquest.com.proxy.nss.udel.edu/newsstand/printviewfile?accountid =10457).

"Off Duty Policeman Shoots Down Killer: Is worst mass killing in US history, mother; wife slain." 1966. *Williamson Daily News*, August 2, pp. 8. Retrieved March 28, 2013(http://news.google.com/newspapers?id=Q49DAAAAIBAJ&sjid=l64MAA AAIBAJ&pg=4974,1968064&dq=houston+mccoy&hl=en).

Parton Jr, Alfred W. 2012. "Delaware State Police Special Operations Response Team." Delaware State Police. Retrieved April 25, 2013(http://dsp.delaware.gov/sort.shtml).

Pocsik, Scott. 2000. *Sheriff's Office Final Report on the Columbine High School Shootings CD.* Golden, Colorado: Jefferson County Sheriff's Office.

"Police Officer Describes Tower Assault." 1966. *The Herald-Tribune*, August 3, pp. 9. Retrieved March 28, 2013 (http://news.google.com/newspapers?id=GiMhAAAAIBAJ&sjid=1mUEAAAAI BAJ&dq=houston%20mccoy&pg=4139%2C357318).

Rast, Bob. 1979. "'Firecrackers' Proved to Be Deadly." *The Madison Courier*, January 31, pp. 9. Retrieved March 28, 2013 (http://news.google.com/newspapers?id=ontbAAAAIBAJ&sjid=6lANAAAAIBAJ&pg= 2206,4754989&dq=firecrackers+proved+to+be+deadly&hl=en).

Recer, Paul. 1966. "Retired Airman, Quick Volunteer." *Corsicana Daily Sun*, August 2, pp. 3. Retrieved March 28, 2013 (newspaperarchive.com).

Recer, Paul. 1966. "Policemen Offer Lives." *Corsicana Daily Sun*, August 2, pp. 1 & 2. Retrieved March 28, 2013 (newspaperarchive.com).

"School Sniper Bragged of 'Something Big to Get on TV'." 1979. *The Evening Independent*, January 30, pp. 2A. Retrieved March 28, 2013 (http://news.google.com/newspapers?id=r8EwAAAAIBAJ&sjid=3VgDAAAAIBAJ&dq=brenda%20spencer&pg=6676%2C3418018).

Scott-Blair, Michael. 1979. "Slain School Men Knew of Danger; Aide Describes Scene of Horror." *The San Diego Union*, January 30, A-9.

Standefer, Jon. 1979. "Sniper Attack Leaves 2 Dead, 9 Hurt in Schoolyard; Girl, 16, Surrenders: Youngsters scramble for their lives in hail of rifle fire." *The San Diego Union*, January 30, A-1 & 8.

"Unsung Hero: Man drives dump truck into school sniper's line of fire." 1979. *The Evening Independent*, February 7, pp. 2A. Retrieved March 28, 2013 (http://news.google.com/newspapers?id=g1pQAAAAIBAJ&sjid=3FgDAAAAIBAJ&dq=brenda%20spencer&pg=5302%2C1493029).

Wolf, Leslie. 1989. "San Carlos Killer Now Making Clothes in Prison: Stockton Tragedy Mirror Spencer Case." *Los Angeles Times*, January 17. Retrieved January 19, 2013 (http://articles.latimes.com/1989-01-18/local/me-486_1_san-carlos).

YouTube. N.d. "Brenda Ann Spencer School Shooting: Part 1-5." Retrieved March 29, 2013(http://www.youtube.com/watch?v=Y9jnQKiLxr0&list=PLz9IPo5JLXHGSmeX3rhcaKl5wCRJvpCaz).

Appendix A
Terms

1. Branch- The organizational level having functional or geographical responsibility for major aspects of incident operations. The branch is organizationally situated between the section chief and the division or group in the operations section, and between sections and units in the logistic section. Branches are identified by the use of roman numerals or by functional areas. (FEMA 2008)

2. Chain of Command- A series of command, control, executive, or management positions in hierarchical order of authority. (FEMA 2008)

3. Command Staff- Consist of public information officer, safety officer, liaison officer, and other positions as required, who report directly to the Incident Commander. They may have an assistant or assistants, as needed. (FEMA 2008)

4. Division- The partition of an incident in geographical areas of operation. Divisions are established when the number of resources exceeds the manageable san of control of the operations chief. A division is located within the Incident Command System organization between the branch and resources in the operation section. (FEMA 2008)

5. General Staff- A group of incident management personnel organized according to function, and reporting to the Incident Commander. The general staff normally consist of the operations section chief, planning section chief, logistics section chief, and financial/administration section chief. An intelligence/investigation chief may be established, if required, to meet incident management needs. (FEMA 2008)

6. Group- Established to divide the incident management structure into functional areas of operation. Groups are composed of resources assembled to perform a special function not necessarily within a single geographic division. Groups, when activated, are located between branches and resources in the operation section. (FEMA 2008)

7. Incident Command- Responsible for overall management of the incident and consists of the incident commander, either singular or unified command, and any assigned supporting staff. (FEMA 2008)

8. Incident Commander (IC) - The individual responsible for all incident activities, including the development of strategies and tactics, and the ordering and release of resources. The IC has overall authority and responsibility for conducting incident

operations, and is responsible for the management of all incident operations at the incident site. (FEMA 2008)

9. Incident Command Post (ICP) - The field location where the primary functions are performed. The ICP may be co-located with the incident base or other incident facilities. (FEMA 2008)

10. Incident Command System (ICS) - A standardized on-scene emergency management construct specifically designed to provide for the adoption of an integrated organizational structure that reflects the complexity and demands of single or multiple incidents, without being hindered by jurisdictional boundaries. ICS is the combination of facilities, equipment, personnel, procedures, and communications operating within a common organizational structure, designed to aid in the management of resources during incidents. It is used for all kinds of emergencies, and is applicable to small as well as large and complex incidents. ICS is used by various jurisdictions and functional agencies, both public and private, to organize field-level incident management operations. (FEMA 2008)

11. Jurisdiction- A range or sphere of authority. Public agencies have jurisdiction at an incident related to their legal responsibilities and authority. Jurisdictional authority at an incident can be political, geographical, or functional. (FEMA 2008)

12. Late 20th Century- Years from 1960 to 1999.

13. Liaison Officer- A member of the command staff responsible for coordinating with representatives from cooperating and assisting agencies or organizations. (FEMA 2008)

14. Logistics- Providing resources and other services to support incident management. (FEMA 2008)

15. Logistics Section- The section responsible for providing facilities, services, and material support for the incident. (FEMA 2008)

16. Mass Murder- Multiple killings in one episode at one location. (Bockler 2013)

17. Mutual Aid and Assistance Agreement- Written or oral agreement between and among agencies/organizations and/or jurisdictions that provides a mechanism to quickly obtain emergency assistance in the form of personnel, equipment, materials, and other associated services. The primary objective is to facilitate rapid, short-term deployment of emergency support prior to, during, and/or after an incident. (FEMA 2008)

18. National Incident Management System (NIMS)- Provides a systematic, proactive approach guiding government agencies at all levels, the private sector, and nongovernmental organizations to work seamlessly to prepare for, prevent, respond to, recover from, and mitigate the effects of incidents regardless of size, cause, location, or complexity in order to reduce the loss of life or property, and harm to the environment. (FEMA 2008)

19. National Response Framework (NRF) - Guides how the nation conducts all hazard response. The framework documents key response principles, roles, and structures that organize national response. It describes how communities, states, federal, private sector, nongovernmental organizations apply these principles for a coordinated, effective national response. It describes special circumstances where the federal government exercises a larger role, including incidents where federal interests are involved and catastrophic incidents where a state would require significant support. It allows first responders, decision makers, and supporting entities to provide a unified national response. (FEMA 2008)

20. Operational Period- The time scheduled for executing a given set of operation actions as specified in the IAP. Operational periods can be of various lengths, although they usually last 12 to 24 hours. (FEMA 2008)

21. Operations Section- The section responsible for all tactical incident operations and implementation of the IAP. In the ICS, it normally includes subordinate branches, divisions, and/or groups. FEMA 2008)

22. Planning Section- The section responsible for the collection, evaluation, and dissemination of operational information related to the incident, and for preparation and documentation of the IAP. This section also maintains information on the current and forecasted situation, and on the status of resources assigned to the incident. (FEMA 2008)

23. Public Information Officer (PIO)- A member of the command staff responsible for interfacing with the public and media, and/or with other agencies, with incident related information. (FEMA 2008)

24. Rampage (noun)- Violent or excited behavior that is reckless, uncontrolled, or destructive. (Collins 2013)

25. Resources- Personnel and major items of equipment, supplies, and facilities available or potentially available for assignment to incident operations and for which status is maintained. Resources are described by kind and type, and may be used in operational

support or supervisory capacities at an incident, or at an emergency operation center. (FEMA 2008)

26. Response- Immediate actions to save lives, protect property and the environment, and meet basic human needs. Response also includes the execution of emergency plans and actions to support short-term recovery. (FEMA 2008)

27. Safety Officer- A member of the command staff responsible for monitoring incident operations, and advising the incident commander on all matters relation to operational safety, including the health and safety of emergency responder personnel. (FEMA 2008)

28. Serial Killing- Multiple killings in distinct episode separated by intervals of time. (Bockler 2013)

29. Spree Killing - Multiple killings in one episode occurring in more than one location. (Bockler 2013)

30. School Shooting/Rampage School Shooting- usually at school or a school-related place by an adolescent who is a current or former student; multiple victims. (Bockler 2013)

31. School- any educational institution or building; a faculty, institution, or department specializing in a particular subject; the staff and pupils of a school; the period of instruction in a school or one session of this; meetings held occasionally for members of a profession, etc; a place or sphere of activity that instructs; a body of people or pupils adhering to a certain set of principles, doctrines, or methods. (Collins 2013)

32. Span of Control- The number of resources for a supervisor is responsible, usually expressed as the ratio of supervisors and individuals. This can be anywhere between 1:3 to 1:7, but the preferred ratio is 1:5. (FEMA 2008)

33. Staging Area- Established for the temporary location of available resources. A staging area can be any location in which personnel, supplies, and equipment can be temporarily housed or parked while awaiting operational assignment. (FEMA 2008)

34. Standardized Emergency Management System (SEMS)- Management of multiagency and multijurisdictional response. (Cal EMA 2013)

35. Task Force- Any combination of resources assembled to support a specific mission or operational need. All resource elements within a task force must have common communications, and a designated leader. (FEMA 2008)

36. Unit- The organizational element with functional responsibility for a specific incident planning, logistic, or finance/administration activity. (FEMA 2008)

37. Special Weapons and Tactical (SWAT)- A police or military unit specially trained and equipped to handle unusually hazardous situations or missions. (Collins 2013)

38. Special Operations Response Team (SORT)- Provides the Division with a tactical response to the following: hostage incidents, armed barricade incidents, high risk warrant service, high risk vehicle stops, dignitary protection, surveillance assistance and any crisis situation deemed appropriate by the Executive Staff. (Parton Jr 2012)

39. Critical Incident Shoot Team (CIST) - Team "of highly trained and skilled investigators, comprised of personnel from each participating law enforcement agency and the District Attorney's Office, be formed to investigate an incident in which any law enforcement officer within the judicial district uses deadly force, or attempts to use deadly force, against a human being while acting under the color of official law enforcement duties. (Pocsik 2000)

40. Triage-the sorting of and allocation of treatment to patients and especially battle and disaster victims according to a system of priorities designed to maximize the number of survivors. (Collins 2013)

41. Homeland Security Presidential Directive Five (HSPD-5)- To prevent, prepare for, respond to, and recover from terrorist attacks, major disasters, and other emergencies, the United States Government shall establish a single, comprehensive approach to domestic incident management. (Bush 2003)

42. Homeland Security Presidential Directive Eight (HSPD-8)- This directive is aimed at strengthening the security and resilience of the United States through systematic preparation for the threats that pose the greatest risk to the security of the Nation, including acts of terrorism, cyber attacks, pandemics, and catastrophic natural disasters. Our national preparedness is the shared responsibility of all levels of government, the private and nonprofit sectors, and individual citizens. Everyone can contribute to safeguarding the Nation from harm. As such, while this directive is intended to galvanize action by the Federal Government, it is also aimed at facilitating an integrated, all-of-Nation, capabilities-based approach to preparedness. (Obama 2011)

Appendix B

August 1, 1966 Tower Sniper Timeline
University of Texas in Austin

Time	Location	Details
12:30am	Penthouse Apartment	Margaret Whitman (mother) already dead
2:05	906 Jewell St, Austin, TX	Kathy Whitman (wife) stabbed to death
7:15	Austin Rental Equipment Service	Rented dolly to carry footlocker to tower observation deck, and then barricade door
11:40	University of Texas in Austin	Arrived on campus
11:44	UTA Tower	Entered 27th floor and killed receptionist
11:47	UTA Tower	Approaching observation deck when a family of six passed him on their descent down the stairs Killed mother and son
11:48	UTA Tower	On observation deck lining up guns for easy maneuvering Block door with dolly Open fires on people below with military-style accuracy and precision UTA security receives 1st report
11:52	Austin PD Headquarters	Receive 1st report Texas Highway Patrol & Texas Rangers responding
12:03pm	UTA Student Center	Occasional sirens heard
12:05	UTA Health Center	On call Dr. called to tower
12:23	UTA campus green	Police & civilians return fire with privately owned deer rifles because police issued weapons are ineffective or restricted Police & civilians are outgunned, outmaneuvered, and pinned down
12:28	UTA Student Center	Sirens become more obvious
12:35	UTA campus green	Armored vehicle used to pickup injured and deceased
12:48	Base of UTA Tower	Austin PD officers Martinez and McCoy start ascending tower with civilian Alan Crum
12:50	Above UTA Tower	Sharpshooter attempts to kill sniper while flying overhead, but fails
1:10	Mall across street from campus	Evacuation starts in area
1:21	UTA Tower	Martinez, McCoy, and Alan Crum enter observation deck
1:24	UTA Tower	Sniper killed

(Barr 2013; Biography 2004; Helmer 2000; Herald Tribune 1966; Lavergne 1997; Lodi News Sentinel 1986; Martinez 2005; Recer 1966; Williamson Daily News 1966)

January 29, 1979 Monday Massacre Timeline
Grover Cleveland Elementary School

Time	Location	Details
8:30am	Grover Cleveland Elementary School	1st bell for class & shooting starts Shooters home 150 ft. across from school, front entrances align Driveway flanked by wing of school and an ivy-covered fence, creating a corridor for the bullets to travel
8:40	San Diego PD Headquarters	Receive 1st report Negotiators, Paul Olsen & Chester Thurston, respond 100+ officers & 20 patrol units respond Security guard from nearby high school respond
8:50	Grover Cleveland Elementary School	Shooting cease after 20 minutes due to phone ringing, it was the reporter covering the incident (coincidental) Approximately 36 rounds Shooters location 150 ft from school Approximately 11 people hit Nearby homes evacuated
9:00	Outside shooter's home Within shooter's home	Standoff begins 6 ½ hrs Phone interview with San Diego Tribune, & then took phone off the hook
10:30	Grover Cleveland Elementary School	Students & teachers evacuated from classrooms & bathrooms
12:00pm	Shooter's home	SWAT getting in position to launch tear gas canisters into home SDPD negotiators (Paul Olsen & Chester Thurston) makes first contact Hang up on negotiator several times
1:20	Grover Cleveland ES	Children evacuated out backdoor of gym to nearby high school
3:00	Shooter's home	Rapport established between shooter and negotiator
3:06	Shooter's home	Shooter surrender's weapons
3:30	Driveway of Shooter's home	Shooter surrenders

(Cannon 1979; Clarke 1979; Cubbison 1979; Fast 2013; Rast 1979; Scott-Blair 1979; Standefer 1979; The Evening Independent 1979; The Madison Courier1979; Wolf 1989; YouTube N.d.)

January 17, 1989 Cleveland School Killings Timeline
Cleveland Elementary School

Time	Location	Details
11:40am	Cleveland Elementary School	Primary recess starts for 300+ 1st through 3rd grade students Shooter enters playground from south and starts firing at students in a spraying motion
11:42am	Cleveland Elementary School	Car explodes and burns
11:42	Stockton PD Headquarters	Received 1st report
11:42	Cleveland Elementary School	Shooter commits suicide with 9mm handgun
11:44	Cleveland Elementary School	Local, County, and federal response
11:45	Stockton PD Headquarters	2 more calls received about shots fired
11:48	Cleveland Elementary School	Stockton PD on scene
11:49	CES	1st victim located
11:54	CES	Shooter located and secured
11:57	CES	Command Post established
12:02pm	Command Post	All area hospital advised, and ambulances requested
12:05	Command Post	Incident Commander starts giving assignments

(Halvorson 1989; Kempsky 1989; Johnson 2013; Los Angeles Times 1989; New York Times 1989)

* Times and information is sketchy because it happened so quickly. Halvorson 1989 material is raw footage by a future reporter.

April 20, 1999 Columbine Shooting Timeline
Columbine High School

Time	Location	Details
11:21am	Wadeworth (street)	Explosion reported (diversion)
11:22	Columbine High School (CHS)	Duffle bag placed in cafeteria (incendiary device) Students begin to notice commotion outside
11:23	Jefferson County Sheriff's Office	Receive 1st report
11:24	CHS	1st officer on scene (JCSO)
11:25	CHS	Shots heard outside of library
11:26	Littleton Fire Dept.	Dispatched to location of explosion (diversion)
11:27	CHS	Officer on scene request assistance Shooters outside library door Two pipe bombs explode in cafeteria
11:29	CHS	Shots fired in library
11:31	CHS	Fire alarm activated
11:32	CHS	Mutual aid requested
11:36	CHS (command post)	Man seen on roof (repairman) Pipe bomb explosion in cafeteria (security camera) Command post established
11:37	Weaver & Pierce (staging)	Littleton FD establish staging area Pipe bomb explosion in cafeteria (security camera)
11:44	CHS	Perimeter established
11:46	CHS (cafeteria)	Duffle bag ignites
11:52	CHS (cafeteria)	Sprinklers are activated
11:53	In route	Jefferson County & Arapahoe bomb squads
11:57	Weaver & Pierce (staging)	Ambulances waiting
12pm	CHS	Shooters in library News helicopter commandeered Armored vehicle sent to rescue injured
12:02	CHS	Jefferson County, Denver, & Littleton SWAT use fire truck to get close to school
12:05	CHS	Littleton FD EMS retrieve

		victim from outside of cafeteria door with cover fire from police Deputy spots students hiding in parking lot & evacuate them to safety Mobile crime lab in route
12:06	CHS	SWAT team (Simmons) reach east entrance SWAT team (Manwaring) proceed to west entrance
12:08	CHS (library)	Shooters commit suicide
12:10	Yukon & Caley (triage)	Triage area established by Littleton FD
12:11	CHS	Man on roof removed
12:14	Weaver & Pierce (staging)	Bomb squads assembled
12:17	CHS (south side)	Armed man approaching school (civilian wanting to assist)
12:19	CHS	SWAT team (Manwaring) approach west entrance
12:25	Leawood Elementary School (LES)	Parents directed to go to school
12:30	LES	SORT dispatched to assist in evacuation of students, & incoming parents
12:39	CHS (command post)	Jefferson County mobile command operational
12:40	CHS	Suspected gas leak reported Request for shut off
12:41	CHS (command post)	SWAT team (Williams) arrives
12:43	CHS	SWAT team (Simmons) call for additional SWAT
12:53	CHS	SWAT team (Simmons) on south side of school
1:00	CHS (command post)	CIST activated
1:05	CHS	SWAT team (Williams) enter through window in teachers lounge because a bomb is at the door
1:09	Roofs of neighboring homes	Sharpshooters in place SWAT teams start general sweep of classrooms SWAT team (Simmons) east to west upper level

		SWAT team (Williams) west to east lower level
1:22	Weaver & Pierce (staging)	Arapahoe SWAT assembled
1:45	LES	SORT arrives
1:57	CHS	SWAT team (Williams) evacuate those found in ceiling
2:08	CHS	Students found in tech lab evacuated
2:12	CHS	SWAT team (Lakewood PD) approach west entrance
2:17	CHS	SWAT team (Williams) split into 2 teams to search classrooms
2:24	CHS	SWAT team (Williams) evacuate students located in music area
2:26	CHS (library)	Person seen hanging outside window
2:29	Harris Residence	Littleton FD requested by bomb squad for gas odor
2:38	CHS (library)	SWAT team (Lakewood PD) use armor vehicle to rescue person hanging out of window
2:40	CHS	Students located in vocal room evacuated
2:42	CHS	Science room evacuated Medical assistance requested for wounded teacher (later deceased)
3:15	CHS	Evacuation complete
3:22	CHS (library)	SWAT team (Williams) arrives
3:25	Harris Residence	Bomb & gas found inside Surrounding neighbors evacuated
3:37	CHS	Bomb squad requested Fresh SWAT teams requested
3:55	CHS (parking lot)	SWAT team (Lakewood PD) spot booby trapped cars
4:00	Harris Residence	Device removed
4:04	CHS	Fire alarm & sprinklers deactivated
4:38	CHS	School cleared Medical assistance enters

(Pocsik 2000)

Appendix C

LAW ENFORCEMENT INCIDENT MANAGEMENT STRUCTURE

FIRE DEPARTMENT INCIDENT MANAGEMENT STRUCTURE

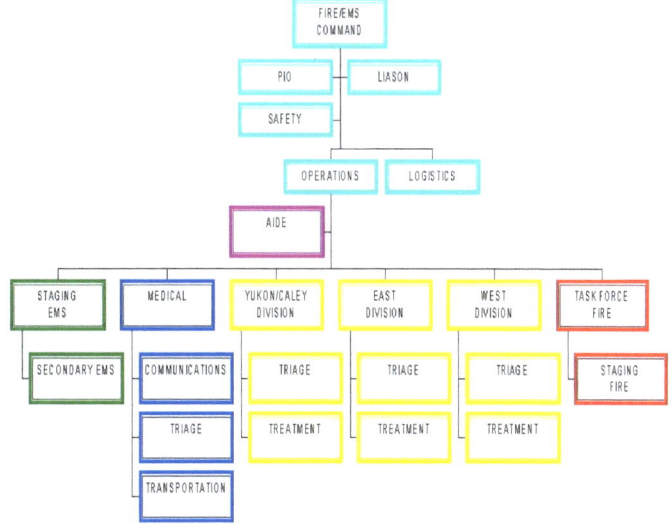

(Pocsik 2000)

www.ingramcontent.com/pod-product-compliance
Lightning Source LLC
Chambersburg PA
CBHW060816290526
45792CB00005BB/1680